Black in White

White face, foreign hands

and other poems from the
Black in White Poetry Competition 2025

CHARLOTTE SHYLLON
+ 24 contributing poets

© Charlotte Shyllon, 2025

First published in 2025 by Paragon Publishing, Rothersthorpe

Cover design: Christine Welby www.1stimpression.org

Front cover illustration: Tia Diana Draws IG: @tiadianadraws

Images used under license from Shutterstock.com

The rights of Charlotte Shyllon to be identified as the author of this work have been asserted by her in accordance with the Copyright, Designs and Patents Act of 1988. The author of each poem included retains the copyright for their individual poems. All rights reserved; no part of this publication may be reproduced, stored in a retrieval system, or transmitted in any form or by any means, electronic, mechanical, including scanning, photocopying, recording or otherwise without the prior written consent of the publisher or a licence permitting copying in the UK issued by the Copyright Licensing Agency Ltd.
www.cla.co.uk

All revenue generated from the sale of this book belongs to The Transforming Words Foundation.

www.ttwf.org.uk

Registered Charity Number: 1213798

ISBN 978-1-78792-109-2

Book design, layout and production management by Into Print
www.intoprint.net

+44 (0)1604 832149

CONTENTS

Dedication & Acknowledgements 6
Foreword by Dame Neslyn Watson-Druée, DBE 7
Introduction by Charlotte Shyllon 10

SECTION 1: Black in White Poetry Competition 2025 13

- Statement About Using Artificial Intelligence Tools
  To Generate Poems   14
- About The Poetry Competition 2025   17
- Meet The Judges   18
- How And Why Our Winners Were Chosen   20
- Our Winners: Workplace Category   21
- Our Winners: Childhood Category   23

SECTION 2: Poems by Charlotte Shyllon 25

- DEI Is For Real   27
- Cut Me Out? Cut It Out!   31
- Flagging Your Feelings   35
- What Do You See?   39
- If I Were White   43

SECTION 3: Guest Poets' Poems 45

- To Be Angry – Tia-zakura   47
- Unboxing – Serena Malcolm   55
- Equality, Diversity, Inclusion & Me… – Poetry Girl   59
- My Name Is Tia – Tia Miles   61

SECTION 4: Winning Poems 2025 – Workplace Category 63

- 1st Prize: White Face, Foreign Hands – Dennis Johnstone   65
- 2nd Prize: What Are Your Plans For The Weekend?
  – Farnaz Rais   71
- 3rd Prize: Leading Lady – Agness F. Nyama   73

SECTION 5: Winning Poems 2025 – Childhood Category 75

- 1st Prize: School Ain't Neutral – Jebril Umo (17 years old)   77
- 2nd Prize: The Day I Stopped Raising My Hand
  – Zachary Andrade (15 years old)   81
- 3rd Prize: Sweets Took On A Different Meaning
  – Jenny Mitchell   85

SECTION 6: Highly Commended Poems 2025 (in alphabetical order) 87

- A Colour That Won't Wash Off – Muntaha [Childhood]   88
- Diversity Hire – Yvonne Dang [Workplace]   90
- Dreams Folded Quiet – Janhvi [Childhood] (15 years old)   92
- Echoes In An Empty Playground
  – Princess Opara [Childhood] (16 years old)   94
- Fragmented Existence – Dr G [Childhood]   98
- How Black – Natasha McDonnell-Tanoh [Childhood]   101
- I Know Who I Am
  – Paarth Aggarwal [Workplace] (16 years old)   104
- My New Colleague – Bill Lythgoe [Workplace]   106
- Prayer – Tavia Panton [Workplace]   107
- She Carries The Silence Differently
  – Debbie Miller [Workplace]   109
- Speak When Spoken Word
  – Jebril Umo [Childhood] (17 years old)   111

- The BAME Game – Farnaz Rais [Workplace]   113
- Tuti – Beda Higgins [Childhood]   114
- What I Carry To Work
  – Ifeoma Q. Opara [Workplace] (17 years old)   115
- Which Allegiance to Which Cunning
  – Shannon Clinton-Copeland [Childhood]   119
- Zero Tolerance – Neelam Sharma [Workplace]   122

SECTION 7: About The Transforming Words Foundation....125

- Know Us   127
- Understand Us   128
- Support Us   129
- Contact Us   131

Dedication

This book, like its predecessors, is dedicated to all those who see and value the benefits of diversity, equity and inclusion, and who labour actively in whatever capacity within this field to help open the minds of those who are the reason why these poems have been written…

Acknowledgements

I would like to acknowledge several people who have been instrumental in helping to compile the contents for this book.

- All the poetry competition entrants, especially those featured in this book. Without their poems, this book wouldn't be as content rich as it is. Not everyone could be selected and celebrated publicly, but we appreciate everyone's efforts.
- Dame Neslyn Watson-Druée, DBE, who kindly wrote the inspiring foreword to this book.
- The guest poets who have allowed us to publish their poems: Tia-zakura Camilleri, Serena Malcolm, Poetry Girl and Tia Miles.
- The judges in the Black in White Poetry Competition 2025 who diligently undertook an iterative judging process to select the winning and highly commended poems: Anni Domingo, Cornelius Alexander, Sonia Brown MBE and Tia-zakura Camilleri.
- The two individuals who carried out the shortlisting: Tia Miles and Zoe Brown.
- The members of The Transforming Words Foundation team who are committed to our common passion project.
- My children, other family members and friends who gave an encouraging word or two along the way or provided support and inspiration.

Most of all, I thank God for giving me the passion, strength and focus to continue on this journey.

FOREWORD

It is a profound privilege to write the foreword for this book. The Black in White Poetry Competition, now in its fifth year, is a dedicated space that provides a vital platform for voices sharing the raw, authentic experiences of racism across all facets of life. From childhood innocence to the complex realities of working life, these poems illuminate personal encounters that speak to a universal struggle rooted in identity, injustice, and resilience. Each year, the collection of poetry published in this anthology not only captures this spectrum of human experience but also acts as a powerful call for awareness, empathy, and societal change. The diversity of backgrounds reflected in the poems demonstrates that racism's reach is broad and deep, touching lives in subtle and overt ways, yet the poems unify these stories through shared truth and collective courage.

What makes this competition particularly outstanding is the way it weaves together individual narratives with technical mastery. The poems are crafted with care, exhibiting polish, skill, and artistry that elevate their message without detracting from their emotional immediacy. This elegant blend of beauty and power reflects the dedication of the poets, who use language as a vessel for education and transformation. They demonstrate that poetry is not just an expressive art form but a form of resistance and a catalyst for change – an emotional toolkit for understanding and confronting societal injustices.

My decision to write this foreword stems from a deep and unwavering belief in poetry's extraordinary capacity to reach the core of the human experience. Poetry possesses an unmatched ability to touch the soul – beyond words alone – acting as a conduit for healing wounds that are often invisible or hard to articulate. Its rhythmic cadence, metaphorical richness, and personal honesty can uplift spirits weighed down by injustice and pain, providing solace and strength to those who need it most. Through poetry, stories of struggle and resilience are transformed into art that resonates far beyond the page, nourishing emotional wellbeing, fostering empathy, and encouraging reflection and action.

Poets such as Charlotte Shyllon exemplify this transformative capacity. Her compelling anthologies – "Here is Your Heart" from 2022 and "Her Locks Unveiled" from 2023 – stand as powerful testaments to poetry's ability to unveil truths beneath external appearances and surface narratives. Her work invites us to look beyond stereotypes and superficial identities, encouraging us to explore the deep wells of resilience, pride, and self-awareness that lie within. The poetry underscores that words are more than art – they are vital tools for collective and individual soul-therapy. Even amidst profound adversity, these verses inspire hope, reminding us that through storytelling and poetic expression, healing can begin.

Engaging with these poems, I hope readers will experience a wide spectrum of emotions – hope and joy, anger and frustration, empathy and solidarity. I want these words to serve as both mirror and window, reflecting personal struggles while opening our minds to the realities of others. Such emotional engagement can foster compassion, understanding, and a sense of shared humanity. I also hope that these poems will motivate action – prompting us to recognise the emotional toll of racial discrimination and to acknowledge the essential healing power of words. Words that challenge, comfort, and inspire are fundamental in creating spaces where difficult conversations can take place and where progress toward racial equity can be nurtured. Sir Andrew Motion, former British Poet Laureate said:

"Poetry is the language that lets us speak the unspeakable, giving voice to our deepest truths and connecting us through shared human experience."

Looking forward, I remain optimistic about the future of race relations. I believe that the courage and honesty of poets and storytellers will continue to be a driving force toward societal change. As poetry persists as a beacon for truth and resilience, it also holds the potential to serve as a source of emotional wellbeing and collective healing. Its ability to articulate complex feelings, foster empathy, and inspire action makes it an invaluable tool in the ongoing journey toward inclusion and understanding. When we embrace these voices – these powerful verses – we take vital steps toward healing societal wounds and building bridges across differences.

One poem at a time, we inch closer to a future rooted in mutual respect, dignity, and genuine connection.

In embracing the voices of these poets and the truths they bravely share, we commit ourselves to a process of ongoing reflection, dialogue, and action. Let us cherish poetry not only as an art form but as a pathway to collective awakening and societal transformation – an enduring reminder that words can heal, empower, and unite us in our shared humanity.

Dame Neslyn Watson-Druée, DBE
Integrity-Centred Leadership | Executive Coach to Senior Leaders | Business Psychologist | Author & Speaker

INTRODUCTION

The Transforming Words Foundation: Sharing Stories, Shaping Societies

Recognition Of Our Mission

Last year, I announced that we were shifting the activities of our social enterprise Back in White into a new charity we had set up called The Transforming Words Foundation (TTWF). I am delighted to confirm that we were entered on the Charity Commission's Register of Charities on 24 June 2025, with the Registered Charity Number 1213798.

Established as a charitable incorporated organisation (CIO), TTWF's objects are: The promotion of equality and diversity for the public benefit in particular but not exclusively by:

- Delivering an annual poetry competition and the publication of poetry collections which allow a wide demographic of people to express and understand the impacts of prejudice and unconscious bias
- Running online poetry workshops, conducting work with schools and other educational institutions and community outreach initiatives.
- Advancing education and raising awareness about the causes, effects and solutions to societal and individual prejudice, racism and unconscious bias.

Our registration as a charity signifies official recognition that there is an ongoing need for organisations like TTWF to operate in this space. We are pursuing our mission of 'sharing stories, shaping societies' with purpose, passion and pride.

Poetry is just one of the methodologies we are employing to achieve this. Yet it remains an important part of what we do at TTWF. It is a powerful means of helping to heal hurts, build resilience, create awareness, encourage understanding, alter mindsets, change behaviours and deliver transformation.

Reason For Our Mission

There are lots of reasons why charities like TTWF are needed. As I meditated on this, one word came clearly to the fore: marginalisation. This was mainly because a couple of recent experiences in the workplace involving marginalisation, which I cover in two of my poems in this book.

The word marginalise is a verb, defined as follows:

- ❖ To relegate to the fringes, out of the mainstream; make seem unimportant. (Collins English Dictionary)
- ❖ To treat someone or something as if they are not important (Cambridge Advanced Learner's Dictionary & Thesaurus)
- ❖ To relegate to an unimportant or powerless position within a society or group (Merriam-Webster Dictionary)

The way Cultural Ally1[1] defines marginalised really resonates with me:

"It refers to people and groups who are pushed away from opportunity, influence, and overall visibility. Today, being marginalised doesn't just mean being excluded. It refers to the systemic ways individuals or communities are treated as less important, less powerful, or less worthy in a variety of areas of life: socially, economically, or politically."

Marginalised groups include people with any of the nine protected characteristics in the Equality Act (2010), not just race. Yet marginalisation of people based on their race is a key reason for our mission.

Many of the poems we have selected as our winning and highly commended entries for inclusion in this book tackle some form of marginalisation. This can be seen across both categories of our competition, occurring in childhood and in the workplace. Experiences of marginalisation are real; they need to be recognised, reported and rejected.

---

1   https://www.cultureally.com/blog/what-does-marginalized-mean-and-why-does-it-matter.

Results Of Our Mission

We need to develop resilience when we face marginalisation. That's the first step to ensuring we are not pulled down into defeat, self-loathing or worse. Resilience comes through a variety of interventions, including the use of transformative words. Resilience is one of the key results we expect our mission to birth – particularly in the hearts and minds of people who experience marginalisation.

I hope you enjoy reading the amazing poems in this book. More than that, I hope they help bring healing and resilience for those who need it and insight and illumination for all.

Please support our mission. You can log onto our website (www.ttwf.org.uk) to donate, or support us via Easyfundraising (www.easyfundraising.org.uk) who provide donations from a wide range of companies when you spend online… in other words, the donations cost you nothing extra. We are just getting started on our journey as a charity and will continue to build and grow – your support will help us to achieve this.

Charlotte Shyllon,
Founder and Chief Executive Officer,
The Transforming Words Foundation

SECTION 1:

Black in White Poetry Competition 2025

Statement About Using Artificial Intelligence Tools to Generate Poems

We are aware that the use of artificial intelligence (AI) tools to generate content has become more commonplace. We have therefore conducted research to enable us to formulate The Transforming Words Foundation's position on how this impacts on the Black in White Poetry Competition.

A research paper published in *Computers in Human Behaviour* in 2021[2] makes some points worthy of consideration. Acknowledging that "projects in which humans and algorithms form hybrid writing teams and collaboratively craft fiction text present one way in which [AI] could enter our daily lives", it questions whether such forms of hybrid collaborations between human and machines should be considered plagiarism. The authors pose some further questions:

To what extent does the creator deserve (financial) credit for the textual outputs?

Would an entry to a poetry competition by a contestant who uses AI input be counted as fraud? If so, how could it be detected? And if not, how should the prize money be split?

Human's ability to detect AI-generated poetry, without the use of AI-detection tools, is part of the issue. An article published in *Nature* in November 2024[3] said that poetry was previously one of the last remaining domains of text in which generative AI language models had not yet reached a high level of "indistinguishability". However, it confirms that "in contrast to previous studies, people are now unable to distinguish AI-generated poetry from the poetry of well-known human poets, being more likely to judge AI-generated poems to be human-written and rating AI-generated poetry more highly along several aesthetic dimensions."

---

2   Nils Köbis, Luca D. Mossink. *Artificial intelligence versus Maya Angelou: Experimental evidence that people cannot differentiate AI-generated from human-written poetry*, Computers in Human Behavior, Volume 114, 2021, 106553, ISSN 0747-5632, https://doi.org/10.1016/j.chb.2020.106553.

3   Porter, B., Machery, E. *AI-generated poetry is indistinguishable from human-written poetry and is rated more favorably*. Sci Rep **14**, 26133 (2024). https://doi.org/10.1038/s41598-024-76900-1.

About the Poetry Competition

Our Position: AI Tools and the Poetry Competition

In reaching our position, we considered that some poetry competitions have chosen to specifically ban AI-generated entries. Based on our research, The Transforming Words Foundation has taken the decision not to do so. We hold the more pragmatic view that a poem can be selected as winning or highly commended using our judging criteria, particularly if its message is potentially transformative and helps to further our mission, whether it was generated by AI or not. Having said this, we accept that individual judges may choose to deduct points from poems if they suspect the use of AI, at their discretion.

Black in White

About the Poetry Competition 2025

The Black in White Poetry Competition is an annual fixture on The Transforming Words Foundation's calendar, launched every year on 21 March, which is World Poetry Day and International Day for the Elimination of Racial Discrimination. It gives people of all races, ethnicities and cultures an opportunity to share some of their experiences or observations of racism in their own voices.

The competition has been running for five years now; the first one opened for entries in July 2021 and was focused on workplace racism. The judging panel selected the winning and highly commended poems, the results were announced in September and two months later our first anthology, now titled *Foreign body*, was launched. Since 2022, we have extended the categories to two – workplace and childhood – and doubled the number of prizes from three to six. The resulting anthologies are launched during the UK's Black History Month celebration every October. The title of each collection is based on the title of the winning poem in the workplace category.

In 2025, we received nearly 120 entries into the poetry competition. They came mainly from poets across the UK, plus a few from other countries around the world. As in previous years, the entries ranged from hurtful to hopeful. The poems were penned by people describing both past and present situations. Some of the poets were directly involved and others were sharing their views or observations. Some were children as young as 12 years old, some were older adults. Together, their poems were a veritable treasure trove of insights, illumination and inspiration!

Shout out to everyone

There were some excellent poems that didn't make it into this book purely because that's the nature of competitions. The judges would like to thank everyone for their entries and encourage all of those not included to keep telling your stories. Your voice is valued, respected and important.

Meet the Judges

The judges who reviewed, scored and selected the winning and highly commended poems this year were:

Charlotte Shyllon

Charlotte is the Founder and CEO of TTWF, the charity established in 2024 to expand and enhance the work of the social enterprise Black in White which ran this Poetry Competition for four years. She is the lead author of the five Black in White anthologies published to date. In 2023, her poem 'What if diseases didn't destroy destinies?' was selected for display at the Battersea Arts Centre. A former pharmacist and journalist, she now works as a senior business leader, communications consultant and EDI expert.

Anni Domingo

Anni is an actress, director, and writer working in radio, TV, films and theatre. She has worked in America, Europe, Africa, Australia and in many theatres around UK. She currently lectures on drama. Her poems and short stories are published in various anthologies. Her first screenplay, 'Blessed Assurance' has just been filmed and will be out later this year. Her debut novel, *Breaking the Maafa Chain*, was first published in September 2021; she is working on a second novel *Ominira* as part of her PhD at King's College London.

Cornelius Alexander

Cornelius is the Head of PR and Comms at Action for Race Equality. He is a former journalist with more than 35 years of experience in public relations. He has worked as a Press Officer at Scotland Yard as well as for the Mayor of London, the Probation Service and the NHS. He received the 2018 Chartered Institute of Public Relation's (CIPR) Sir Stephen Tallents Medal for Outstanding Contribution to PR and is the BME PR Pros' 2024 Industry Legend. He has worked for 15 years on the CIPR's Diversity and Inclusion initiative and chaired its Diversity Working Group (2010–2013).

About the Poetry Competition

Sonia Brown MBE
Sonia is a multi-award-winning and passionate advocate for women in enterprise and inclusive economic development. She is the visionary founder of the National Black Women's Network (NBWN), launched in 1999. As a recognised authority in business, leadership, marketing and diversity, equity and inclusion, she continues to shape conversations and drive change. She shares insights across radio, podcasts, magazines and national media, championing equity, enterprise and female empowerment.

Tia-zakura Camilleri
Tia is an interdisciplinary creative based in Cardiff who blends poetry, theatre-making, and journalism as powerful tools for activism. Best known for her rhythmic approach to 'flowetry', she performs her spoken-word pieces on stages across the UK. First published at 18 years old, she is driven by a deep passion for community and dedicated to making poetry more accessible to young, marginalised groups by delivering interactive workshops that inspire and empower the next generation of storyteller.

How and Why Our Winners Were Chosen

The judging process

Every year we follow a rigorous judging process. We convene a judging panel to review and score the poems. We bring new judges on board every year; some are poets themselves, some from other backgrounds. The mix of perspectives makes for a well-rounded and inclusive approach.

The process commences with shortlisting stage because we receive too many poems to ask our judges to review. This year, shortlisting was carried out by two independent individuals, poet and illustrator Tia Miles and PhD researcher at the University of Oxford Zoe Brown.

The shortlisted entries were then sent to the judges, who reviewed all the entries anonymously. This involved a detailed initial sift and first round scoring of the shortlisted poems by each judge individually against six criteria:

1) beauty, power, education or entertainment; 2) technical excellence; 3) form and flow; 4) choice of words and readability; 5) polish and expertise; and 6) overall impact.

The judges' individual scores were summarised and the poems listed in order based on the total scores they receive. The judges then reviewed and discussed this allocation together in a final online judging session to ensure that the winning and highly commended selections exemplify the competition's objectives. They selected the 1st, 2nd and 3rd placed winners in both categories, and 16 poems as highly commended.

The judges chose the winners in both categories from the rich repository of rhymes received with difficulty! The final judging sessions lasted two hours and we made good use of every minute. We carefully considered and aligned on our choice of the top three poems in the two categories, then looked briefly at the highly commended entries to ensure there were no issues. The rationale for selecting our winners is explained below.

About the Poetry Competition

Our Winners: Workplace Category

❖ **1st PRIZE**

White Face, Foreign Hands – Dennis Johnstone

This poem looks deeply at issues like race, class, migration, and the hidden work that keeps society running. It takes place in the break room of a care setting and focuses on immigrant healthcare workers – men and women from former colonies – who look after elderly people in Britain. The poem is written via the lens of a white foreigner who blends in as British, who thinks about how his skin colour and accent give him privileges that contrast with the marginalisation faced by his coworkers. Using strong images and quiet anger, the poem shows how colonial history still affects people today, how racism casually shows up in everyday life, and how hard it can be to feel like you belong. It is a powerful reflection on identity, history, and the quiet strength of those who support a country that often overlooks them.

❖ **2nd PRIZE**

What Are Your Plans For The Weekend? – Farnaz Rais

A powerful reflection on cultural appropriation and microaggressions, this poem speaks to the emotional toll of being othered in everyday interactions. Through the lens of a casual workplace conversation, it exposes how elements of one's heritage – spiritual practices, traditional foods, clothing and beauty rituals – are celebrated when adopted by white peers but mocked or misunderstood when expressed by those to whom they truly belong. The poem captures the quiet frustration of watching one's culture be commodified and sanitised, while your own lived experience is dismissed or erased. It is a poignant critique of how white standards often dictate what is considered refined, acceptable, or "aesthetic," leaving one caught between pride and pain.

Black in White

❖ 3rd PRIZE
Leading Lady – Agness F. Nyama

This bold and unapologetic poem calls out tokenism, fake diversity and industries that use identity as a marketing tool, claiming to be inclusive. The poet speaks out against being reduced to stereotypes, treated like a quota, or used to fit a certain image. With sharp words and strong rhythm, she refuses to stay silent or play along. She refuses to be a brand, a trend, or a checkbox. The poem shows the struggle between being seen and being ignored, and it challenges shallow efforts at inclusion that do not fix deeper systemic problems. It is a powerful statement of self-worth that will not shrink to make others comfortable.

About the Poetry Competition

Our Winners: Childhood Category

❖ **1ˢᵗ PRIZE**

School Ain't Neutral – Jebril Umo (17 years old)

This powerful poem shares the story of a young Black student moving through the British school system, revealing its hidden prejudices and contradictions. Each section is shaped like a school subject or moment, showing how the student's identity is often mispronounced, misunderstood, and marginalised. It highlights everyday racism from teachers and shallow efforts at inclusion, showing how schools can limit rather than support Black talent. Through resistance and self-reflection, the poet reclaims control, refusing to be shaped by others' views. The final lines turn survival into victory, boldly claiming their voice and rewriting their story. It is more than a critique – it is a statement of self-ownership.

❖ **2ⁿᵈ PRIZE**

The Day I Stopped Raising My Hand – Zachary Andrade (15 years old)

This poem is a deeply personal reflection on the quiet wounds of childhood exclusion, microaggressions and racial bias within the classroom. Through vivid imagery and rhythmic storytelling, the poet recounts how their early enthusiasm and brilliance were gradually dimmed by dismissive teachers, unequal praise, and cultural insensitivity. The poem captures the pain of being overlooked, mocked, and misunderstood – not just academically, but culturally and emotionally. Yet it ends with a powerful reclamation: the act of writing becomes a raised hand, a defiant gesture of self-worth and solidarity. It is a tribute to every child whose light was dimmed, and a reminder that their brilliance was never the problem – it was the system that failed to see it.

❖ **3rd PRIZE**

Sweets Took On A Different Meaning – Jenny Mitchell

Using sweets and confectionery as a powerful metaphor, this poem explores the painful experiences of growing up as a racialised child in Britain. It shows how childhood, often seen as innocent and joyful, can be marked by racism, exclusion, and trauma. The playful images of playgrounds and treats are set against harsh realities like bullying, slurs, and adult hostility. Each verse turns familiar sweets into symbols of hurt, difference and survival. The poem challenges the idealised view of British childhood, exposing the hidden pain beneath its cheerful surface. It is a moving reflection on identity, memory and the loss of safety in places meant to feel safe.

★★★ **Well done to all our winners!** ★★★

SECTION 2:

Poems by Charlotte Shyllon

DEI Is For Real

Cut Me Out? Cut It Out!

Flagging Your Feelings

What Do You See?

If I Were White

DEI IS FOR REAL

By Charlotte Shyllon

You ought to know better
You should be a path-setter
You claim to be DEI-smart
To pull together, not pull apart.

You always wave the EDI flag
You seem to have it in the bag
You appear to be right on side
To walk aright, with purpose and pride.

But…

You shared a recommendation and left me out
You did it knowingly, without a doubt
You didn't reckon on my ally's insight
She brought your slight into the light.

My ally and I lead together
Linked, conjoined, like in a tether.
She speaks up more, I must confess
I listen more; doesn't make me less.

Excluding me was just not cool
You didn't look smart, you looked the fool.
At first, all I did was sigh
I felt disrespected, and wondered why.

But…

Then my resilience came to the fore
I chose to act, not to feel sore
I called it out to those in the know
This thing is for real, not just for show.

At the next meeting, I made it clear
I spoke up boldly so you would hear
That my role was not just to tick a box
Or because I wear my hair in locs.

I got the gig because I know my stuff
Like it or not, that's just tough.
It doesn't matter what you think or feel
I just hope you know DEI is for real.

Quotable Quotes

"True belonging only happens when we present our authentic, imperfect selves to the world. Our sense of belonging can never be greater than our level of self-acceptance."

Brene Brown

Black in White

CUT ME OUT? CUT IT OUT!

By Charlotte Shyllon

You're one of our vendors
You compiled a submission for us
Then decided I shouldn't see it.
You said it was 'sensitive'
Because it contained salary details.
How on earth could you think
It was okay to cut me out?
Cut it out!

I could understand if I was junior
But not only am I a senior bod,
I also have a seat on the Board.
I'm the one who gets to sign off
On the work that you do.
So how on earth could you think
It was okay to cut me out?
Cut it out!

You sent the work in for approval
You shared it with our finance person
Who, by the way, reports to me.
You didn't think I'd know
But unlike you they know I need to know.
How on earth could you think
It was okay to cut me out?
Cut it out!

Black in White

When I found out of course I was cross
Such disrespect for me as the boss.
Especially as you'd dismissed my request for speed
But caved in when my boss pressed the need.
I asked myself 'Are they always so slack?',
Then the eternal question: 'is it because I'm Black?'
Who knows… but one thing I am clear about
Is that it's not okay to cut me out;
Cut it out!

Quotable Quotes

"To know the true reality of yourself, you must be aware not only of your conscious thoughts, but also of your unconscious prejudices, bias and habits."

Unknown

Black in White

FLAGGING YOUR FEELINGS

By Charlotte Shyllon

Flags are popping up everywhere,
Union Jacks, George Crosses, here and there.
It's a clear sign to all the non-whites
You want to deprive us of our rights.
You say this is mainly about the migrants.
They come here fleeing poverty and tyrants.
You fail to see some are escaping danger,
Instead all you feel is stranger danger.

You fear an invasion, a takeover of whiteness,
All you see is difference and darkness.
Your feelings are getting the better of you
So you are showcasing the red, white and blue.
Flagging your feelings is a visible display
You hope your flag will help you say
That migrants are not welcome here
Don't care at all if you're spreading fear.

Part of the problem was colonisation
Added to that is globalisation
Migration isn't something anyone foresaw
Or the movement of people fleeing war.
I've been living here for 50+ years
But I see the flags, and fight back tears
For British-born non-whites, terrified, scared
Technically natives, but not… it must be weird.

Black in White

Even in schools they don't feel safe
Some feel alone, like an unwanted waif.
With racist incidents on the rise
We console our kids, calming their cries.
You want Reform to lead the way
Hoping to see a brighter day
Flagging your feelings to 'foreigners' who stay
Flagging that you want us to go away.

What happens next is still unclear
For now we all continue to live in fear;
You fear that you are losing the fight
We fear that we are losing the right.
All we can do is watch and wait
Hoping for a lessening of the hate
Hoping one day the flags disappear
And acceptance replaces all the fear.

Defining Moment: Reverse Racism

Also referred to as '**reverse discrimination**', **reverse racism** is the perceived racism or discrimination that is said to occur against a dominant group or political majority, resulting from policies and practices that are intended to level the playing field and remove barriers for minority ethnic groups. This term is commonly used by detractors of positive or affirmative action, who believe that these policies cause members of traditionally dominant groups to be discriminated against.

Source: University of Washington – School of Public Health – ED&I Glossary

Black in White

WHAT DO YOU SEE?

By Charlotte Shyllon

When you look at me,
What do you see?
Do you see all of me?
Or just this dark skin that covers me?

When I start to speak,
Do you hear me?
Or does your mind start to freak
At the accent that comes forth from me?

When you ask me my name,
Is it something you're used to?
Or if it's unusual, not the same,
Do you cringe and baulk at that too?

When you see my afro hair,
Do you think it looks strange?
Do you fuss, fret or fear,
And hope that tomorrow it'll change?

When I wear a bright dress,
Does 'It works on your skin tone' mean it's too strong?
Should the business look be subtler, something less?
Are dark clothes right, but dark skin wrong?

No! No! No! When you look at me
See all of me.
I am more than my clothes, hair, name, accent, skin;
And underneath the skin, we are kin.

+++

Originally published in Black in White, 2020

Poems by Charlotte Shyllon

Defining Moment: Anti-Racism

Anti-Racism is defined as the work of actively opposing racism by advocating for changes in political, economic and social life that would dismantle racist processes and attitudes. An **anti-racist** is someone who actively supports anti-racist policies, processes, practices, ideas and attitudes via their actions. Racism is a powerful collection of racist policies that lead to racial inequity and are substantiated by racist ideas. Antiracism is a powerful collection of antiracist policies that lead to racial equity and are substantiated by antiracist ideas.

Source: Ibram Kendi

Black in White

IF I WERE WHITE

By Charlotte Shyllon

Don't misunderstand me… I love being Black,
But sometimes I wonder if it has held me back.
Would clients and colleagues be more complimentary about me,
If I were white?

Maybe it's just a chemistry thing;
Maybe it's because sometimes *I* hold myself back and lack zing.
But would you have taken to me like you took to him,
If I were white?

I have never considered myself to be less.
I was raised rather privileged, I must confess.
But would I have made it further up the career ladder,
If I were white?

When you asked me if my parents were proud of me
Because, I guess, you'd assumed they were C2DE*.
Would you have viewed me as your socio-economic equal,
If I were white?

As we chatted, you asked where I was from, and I sighed;
I thought that type of question had long since died.
I'm British, like you, but explained my ancestry; would I have had to,
If I were white?

Black in White

I visited a swish restaurant I'd been to with white colleagues many times before;
But this time, when I went with a Black friend, the service was poor.
Just an off day? Perhaps. But would I be left wondering if it was that or 'something else',
If I were white?

If I had a magic wand and could change my colour, I wouldn't.
Even though it *has* caused me extra stress, I couldn't.
Because one thing I know for sure is that I wouldn't be wonderful me,
If I were white.

* C2DE: Socio-economic grading based on a system of demographic classification. The grades are often grouped into ABC1 and C2DE which equate to middle class and working class, respectively.

+++
Originally published in Black in White, 2020

SECTION 3:
Guest Poets' Poems

To be Angry – Tia-zakura

Unboxing – Serena Malcolm

Equality, Diversity, Inclusion & Me... – Poetry Girl

My Name Is Tia – Tia Miles

Black in White

TO BE ANGRY

By Tia-zakura

I am an angry Black woman.
I am an angry Black woman – I'll admit.
No, not because I choose to submit
to the stereotypes you put over me,
but because I'm conscious.

And I don't believe
you can really separate the two –
to be conscious and not angry.

After I withstand the demanding,
For pandering into your palette,
handed my sentences to you gently,
parcelled in brown boxes marked *fragile*.

Held hostage,
the thoughts of my agile mind
feared being too hostile –
just to find
you don't colour anger with red,
but Black.

I realised that
when Jack got praise
for being confident enough
to raise issue with the ways
in which we strategise management –
for being a pioneer for change,
for being so brave
to challenge the way things are.

But when I disagreed
with part of your policy,
you went and complained to HR
like I'm a troublemaker,
rule-breaker, mood-shaker.
No time for small talk about rugby, eh?
A no faker.
A radical.
Unaffable.
Damnable.
Won't cater.
Can't shape you
or make me tractable.

Trying to keep me captive
in your manacles
constructed of tactical threats
to keep me palatable.
No stress – I'm thinking rational
when I dress too casual,
when I wear my hair so magical
it's "distracting" in the workplace.
You're saying it's impractical.

This is targeted exclusion
hidden in illusions.
You hide from the taboo
Rest and nests
of empty efforts to include.

So why the comments on my attitude?
That I wouldn't wanna mess with you?
I could shuck and jive,
But one step out of line –
You'd still call me aggressive too.

Maybe the EDI training
ain't really doing much.
Anti-racism action plan
ain't coming in clutch.

I guess it's just a sticker
that will secure you some grants
'cause you'll take the money
to work with my community,
but you just can't seem
to diversify your staff.
And then you'll go and call us
"hard to reach"
when you just never let us in the room.
So you lost us.
And we weren't going to relish
in the scraps that you tossed us –
a month for our history,
a few Black writers on your shelves,
taking all our contributions
and keeping it for yourselves.
Shall a Black woman not be angry

Black in White

when the standard that's held
is that our features can be pretty
as long as they sell?

That I should rip the edges from my head
until my scalp bleeds,
and it drips down to my eyes
and I can no longer see –
it seeps down to my mouth,
and then it reaches my feet,
and each inch of me
is covered completely in blood.

Will I be less of a threat
if "Red" to you means *love*?

I used to avoid getting mad.
How wrong it be for me to experience that emotion
to see injustice in my face
and then to cause commotion?

Artifacts and gold – stolen.
Black family unit – broken.
Cut our mother tongues
to hear wagwans in the suburbs spoken.

It's a joke ting, my devotion
can only coexist with hoping
that the power of the people
will lead to overthrowing
the people in power.

But from history, I'm knowing
that power doesn't back up

in the face of kindness.

It's the knowledge.
It's the history.
It's the anger that binds us.

And the blindness to the fact
that they will never get behind us
is why some of us
still parade happily in red lines.

Why do you think anger
is the thing they've chosen to penalise?
I wonder why.

I guess they prefer cries –
because when people are sad,
they don't do anything.
But when we're angry,
we bring about change.

So I'll take that anger,
convert it to the page
and take it to the stage,
in the syllables,
the soliloquies,
the messages I convey.

And when you turn around and say
my poetry is *preachy*,
I'll tell you:
my poetry is to *teach thee*.
White people
And reach we, my people –

let us speak, see (no?)

Why would I use my platform
for anything other than the cause?
To talk about tree, skies, sex, or tidal shores?
Sure – I can write the lines
that will ensure the applause.

But I'm not sure
that's the path my heart was made for.

You might get bored
with my anti-war
and F-the-law discourse.
So you might choose to ignore.
But did I choose to endure
the constant repercussions
of societal flaws?

I guess I've got a strong jaw –
because I will talk and talk and talk and talk
until I cannot talk no more.

And you say you don't get involved,
said you find it exhausting.
So the problem remains unsolved.
So when I can't talk, I'll sing.
And when you rip apart the box
and repurpose the *fragile* tape
to cover my mouth –
I will walk and walk and walk and walk
until I pass out.

I am an angry Black woman.
And not because I'm Black,
but because I'm conscious.

Conscious of the fact I'm Black.
And conscious of the world around me.

It only takes a second to look at the state we're in and see,
really, we should all be angry.

+++
©Tia-zakura 2025
Cardiff-based director, facilitator, spoken-word poet
Insta: @tiazakura

Black in White

UNBOXING

By Serena Malcolm

It's the last day of September,
and I'm just now waking up,
Stirring inside my plastic box,
I'm dusting myself off,
Ready for the stroke of midnight when I get to be:

Black again!

No more pretence,
As I jump down off my shelf,
Straighten myself up,
Quickly check in the mirror that this melanin still pops,
Because it's a terribly dark balcony that houses my box:

334 days with no drop of sun,
With no one daring to look my way,
To hold my gaze,
To acknowledge my shade,
To have the courage to say *anything* positive about the colour of my skin,
Ah, but within the safety of the next 31 days and the bravery it brings?

Well, now, this caged bird gets to sing!

Black in White

Apparently, now it's okay to be me,
I'm allowed now to bow to 90 degrees,
To become the tick that they so desperately need me to be,
Need to see in that box
Not my box, oh no,
The one that shows them to be

The epitome of diversity - don't you know?

They wheel me out like their very own, bespoke, one-woman, EDI show!

Tokenised by 'allies' I haven't spoken to all year,
Who woke *me* up just so that *they* can be woke?
To paper over 334 days of inappropriate jokes?
They wind me up and then watch me go,
Pull my cord and hear me crow,
Oohing at my rhymes and *ahhing* at my prose.

But I know all the while they watch that clock,
Signalling that I need to hurry myself up,
And quickly grab every true ally from this melting pot,
Before they run down the clock and my time is up,
They lie poised and ready to usher me to stop,
To herd me back inside my box,
At 11:59pm on that last day of October,
Faces solemn and reflections sober,
But secretly, they're all glad that it's over.

They now breathe a sigh with conscience cleared,
As again, my pigment appears to disappear,
Like a conveniently chameleonic veneer,
Like a two-way mirror
I can see out, but they can no longer see in here?
So I'm reboxed and reshelved like some cult souvenir.

Well that is, of course, until next year!

+++
©Serena Malcolm 2025
Poet & Storyteller
serenamalcolm.co.uk
linktr.ee/serenamalcolm

Black in White

Guest Poets' Poems

EQUALITY, DIVERSITY, INCLUSION & ME...

By Poetry Girl

I've worked in global spaces,
With different races and many faces...
The more diverse the workforce community seems to be, the less diverse is the reality!

1st strike, I'm a woman, 2nd strike, I'm not white, I wonder what the 3rd strike could be about...
Monday to Friday, I pretend not to be me, only on Saturday and Sunday can I truly be free...
My face doesn't fit, maybe that's it... It always seems like I have to be smarter, I need to be stronger, and what's more, I have to work for longer.

I wonder if there'll ever be true equality, is diversity a pipe dream, does inclusion include me? A level playing field is all I need. I should be able to talk to a Black colleague, without feeling the accusing stares boring into my soul.
Feeling like I need to circulate but I gravitate to those to whom I can relate...

+++
©Poetry Girl 2021
2nd Prize Winner, Black in White Poetry Competition 2021.
Originally published in Black in White's 'Foreign Body'. Reprinted with permission.

Black in White

MY NAME IS TIA

By Tia Miles

I don't want to call this my story, but I have some things to say. I'll start with who I am, a mixed-race girl from the slums. I grew up in a council flat with my sister and my mum. Who's white by the way, like the whitest woman you'll meet. Who says things like "Cor blimey, I'm hank Marvin! Should we get something to eat?"

My dad's no different when I think about it. But my dad is **Black**. Born in the 60's which let's face it, is a different complication.

Because he came from a generation
of people born with aggravation
because his roots are segregation
all caused by pigmentation.

And there's me, a 50/50 mix of both.

"You sound really posh for a Black girl you know". "The way you carry yourself it really doesn't show". "Which one of your parents is Black? Your dad?" "Did your mum raise you alone? It can't be that bad". "Where are you from?". "I mean your parents?" "You can't be British… cause you're **BLACK**".

Where do I stand? Because I don't "sound Black", I don't "act Black" but I sure do look it.

So tell me – is it my curly hair, tanned skin or my "negro nose", that makes you think I should go straight back to the country in which my grandfather rose, just because I'm **Black**?

That drink, you threw at me that night, out of pure spite because I'm not white. How do you think that made me feel? Do you now understand that racism is real?

Where do I stand?

Melanin – The pigment responsible for the darkness of the skin, hair, and eyes.

I have more melanin than you do, but does that make it a crime?

My name is Tia Miles.

+++

©Tia Miles 2020

Contact Tia: IG: @tiadiana_draws

Originally published in Black in White's ' Foreign Body'. Reprinted with permission.

SECTION 4:

Winning Poems 2025 – Workplace Category

1st prize: White Face, Foreign Hands
– Dennis Johnstone

2nd prize: What Are Your Plans For The Weekend?
– Farnaz Rais

3rd prize: Leading Lady
– Agness F. Nyama

Black in White

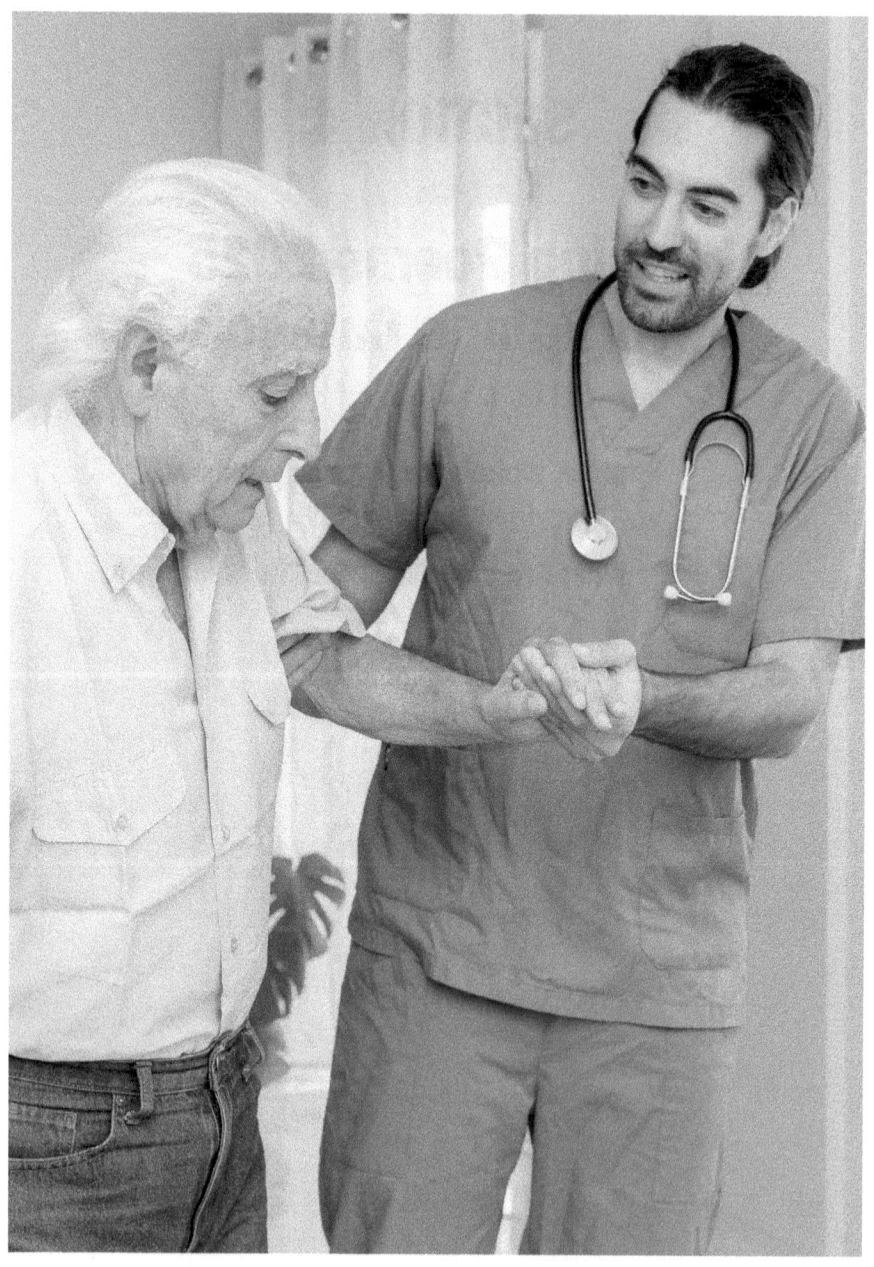

Winning Poems

1ST PRIZE

WHITE FACE, FOREIGN HANDS

By Dennis Johnstone

Break room, day shift – lukewarm tea,
fluorescent hum, creak of tired bones.
She's from Guyana, Nigeria, India,
the Philippines,
and she is from nowhere –
a Palestinian with nothing left
but a name and a history no one wants to hear.

The door swings open – another enters,
brown hands, black hair,
another Indian, another accent,
another body filling the spaces left
by those who wouldn't take the job.

And me –
white, male, passing.
Not British,
but close enough for the ageing ear.
A colonial drawl – relic of empire –
grants me ease denied to them.

Down the corridor, I see her,
another white face, but not like mine.
Polish syllables weigh heavy on her tongue,
marking her foreign in ways I am not.
They hear me and assume I belong.
They hear her and know she does not.

Black in White

Yet here we are,
we who clean them, lift them, hold them steady,
bear witness to their broken bodies,
their cracked voices,
their gratitude, quiet, occasional,
their resentment, quiet, constant.

We take their secrets, their smells, their messes,
we patch them up, prop them up,
wrap their wounds,
and still,
we are thieves in their eyes.

We steal jobs.
We steal benefits.
We steal services.
We steal the future of their sons and daughters.
We drink deep from ancestral wells
without giving thanks.

It is not fact,
but it is their truth.
It cannot be denied.

And the men – ah yes, the men.
Some dismissive, some indifferent,
some with the hunger of old ghosts in their eyes.
They speak of the black and brown women
as if they are furniture,
as if they are souvenirs
from a tour of duty, a posting, a contract abroad.

The worst of the worst
spent years in Africa, in Asia, in places
where they could take without consequence.
The way they watch,
the way they let slip, in unguarded moments,
the things they once did,
the things they wish they still could.

And the Scots –
loud in their exception,
proud in not being English.
But history echoes everywhere.
Colonial ghosts are not English only.

I am a spy,
a white face in a blue tunic,
listening, collecting, knowing.
My colleagues see the shifts in posture,
the flickers of meaning lost in dialect.
I hear the words.
I catch the import.
I feel the depth
of what should never be spoken.

And yet, we stay.
Brown hands, black hands, pale hands
hands from all corners of the earth
holding this country together,
keeping its mothers and fathers alive,
tending to their last days,
wrapping them with care
while they whisper their fears
of a world we already live in.

And me –
white, foreign,
but close enough to pass.
Passing through.
Passing among.
Holding the burden
of all that has passed
and all that still lingers.

Defining Moment: Covert Racism

Refers to racist ideas, attitudes or beliefs expressed in a subtle, hidden or secretive way. **Covert racism** is similar to micro-aggressions in that it often represents a form of racism that remains unchallenged due to it being harder to identify and not always appearing to be racist by intent. Covert racism can manifest via indirect and less blatant comments or behaviours that are seemingly unrelated to an individual's race or ethnicity.

Source: University of York – Glossary of EDI Terminology – Race and ethnicity

Black in White

Winning Poems

2ND PRIZE

WHAT ARE YOUR PLANS FOR THE WEEKEND?
By Farnaz Rais

"What are your plans for the weekend?" they ask.
"Nothing exciting, what about you?" I reply, getting ready to mask
My frustrations, knowing what's coming next
And I hear all about your yoga class and how you flexed
Designer leggings and how fit you have become
But I hear nothing of your drishti or your mind and breath as one.
You tell me about your curry nights, too
And how much you love 'naan bread' and sag aloo
And I don't have the heart to tell you that you just said 'bread bread'
And how you don't eat it separately from curry, but I'll leave that unsaid.
You tell me of your 'Scandinavian scarf dress'
And how that long piece of fabric has you impressed
And I'll feel the pang of what was taken from my culture
Reminded of the embarrassment I felt when my worlds blurred
As we wore intricate lehengas and dupattas at family events
And if by chance we were seen, to you it made no sense.
You talk as you sip your 'chai tea' or 'golden turmeric milk'
But saying 'chai tea' is saying 'tea tea' and is lost on your ilk
And your 'golden milk' goes back through generations of my family
The earthy warmth of that healer against all malady.
And to see your 'clean girl aesthetic' I really can't bear
Because the oil in your hair was the oil in my hair
But they made fun of me at school for the grease in my curls
Because somehow your whiter version of my world
Is more palatable than mine.
Your balance is exotic and mine is unrefined.

Black in White

Winning Poems

3ʳᵈ PRIZE

LEADING LADY

By Agness F. Nyama

this industry
looks at me
sideways

it
sees value
in this (blackbrownbody)
curled only in
stereotypes

unfortunately
for me
I ain't got
the patience

to co-sign your
micro-aggressions
with my silence.

I ain't your
token queen

your diversity hire
to fill your quotas

you checking
your boxes
while measuring
MY worth

with your
tight smiles
and
piercing eyes

[*this ain't no auction block*}
i refuse
to reduce
myself

to fit inside
a [focus group]
a marketing plan
a "look"

this industry
sees me
but
it don't want
to see me

it squints,
cuz my light

got too much
brightness

and it simply
cannot handle
the glare

(*oh sucks*)

i

am what…?

i ain't got
no brand

and i ain't
campaigning
for inclusion
no,
i ain't
a trend
you can post
then forget

#oscarssowhite

(*girl, please*)

Defining Moment: Institutional Racism

Institutional racism also known as '**structural racism**', institutional racism refers specifically to the ways in which institutional policies and practices create different outcomes for different racial groups. The institutional policies may never mention a particular racial group, but their effect is to create proportionate advantages for some ethnic groups, most often white, and oppression or disadvantage for people from minoritised ethnicities.

Source: University of Washington – School of Public Health – ED&I Glossary

SECTION 5:
Winning Poems 2025 – Childhood Category

1st prize: School Ain't Neutral
– Jebril Umo (17 years old)

2nd prize: The Day I Stopped Raising My Hand
– Zachary Andrade (15 years old)

3rd prize: Sweets Took On A Different Meaning
– Jenny Mitchell

Black in White

1ST PRIZE

SCHOOL AIN'T NEUTRAL
By Jebril Umo (17 years old)

I. Roll Call
They butchered my name on the first day.
Didn't even flinch. Didn't ask. Just skipped syllables like parts of me weren't worth pronouncing.
And when I corrected them, they laughed. *"Exotic,"* one said.
As if I was a dish to be tasted, not a boy with history braided into each vowel.

II. Geography
They taught me the capital of Ghana, but never told me why half my aunties speak English with a tongue that folds like apology.
They passed round maps but never mentioned how the borders were carved with bayonets. The only empire we studied was theirs.

III. Uniform Policy
No durags. No braids. No fades too sharp. My hair a disruption. My skin a distraction.
But Tommy's mullet? *"Expressive."* Ellie's nose ring? *"Individuality."*
My culture came with detention slips, theirs came with encouragement.

IV. History
They showed me Rosa, but never Malcolm.
Said Martin had a dream but never told me how that dream ended.
They fed me Civil Rights. with a British accent like racism was an import we politely declined.

V. Parents' Evening

They said I was "easily led." "Mature, but not quite academic." They said I "lacked focus."

Translation: *We don't know what to do with a mind like his, so we'll mould it into something manageable.*

My mum came dressed in pride. They spoke to her like she couldn't read the report between the lines.

VI. Breaktime

I learned quick: Not to speak pidgin too loud. Not to run too fast. Not to argue too smart.

They could mock my lips, my food, my slang, but the minute I fired back *"Aggressive." "Hostile." "Troublemaker."* And suddenly, I wasn't joking anymore.

VII. English Literature

They made us read Of Mice and Men and flinched when I read Crooks' lines too well.

Said I brought "attitude" to the character.

As if I didn't know what it meant to be touched with gloves or left out the stable.

Asked me to analyse pain, but never asked if I recognised it.

VIII. Assembly

Black History Month came like a guest speaker, loud for a day, gone by lunch.

They played Stormzy like it was enough. They let us clap for Marcus Rashford but still served us the coldest meals when we were too hungry to perform.

IX. Final Exam

I wasn't taught, I was targeted, profiled in real time, graded before I wrote a word.
Sat in rooms where the ceiling was lowered just for me, and still they wondered why I stopped raising my hand.

They said: *Well-spoken.* I say: *Well-survived.* They gave me detentions. I gave them dissertations on how to exist in spaces that shrink you and still leave with your rhythm intact. I read between their silences. Wrote in margins. Took notes on everything they didn't say, then said it better. They taught me how to take a test. I taught myself how to name a system, dissect it, and never beg it for approval. So no I didn't just pass. I *well exceeded.* Not just their expectations but my own. Not just the grade boundary but the one they set on my brilliance. I am not your predicted. I am proof that you cannot stream spirit. That you cannot set targets on a child who comes from lineages of fire and forge. Your reports were wrong. Your projections missed. I'm not your success story. I'm my own curriculum. And trust me... **I've already marked your system:**

Incomplete. Needs revision.

Black in White

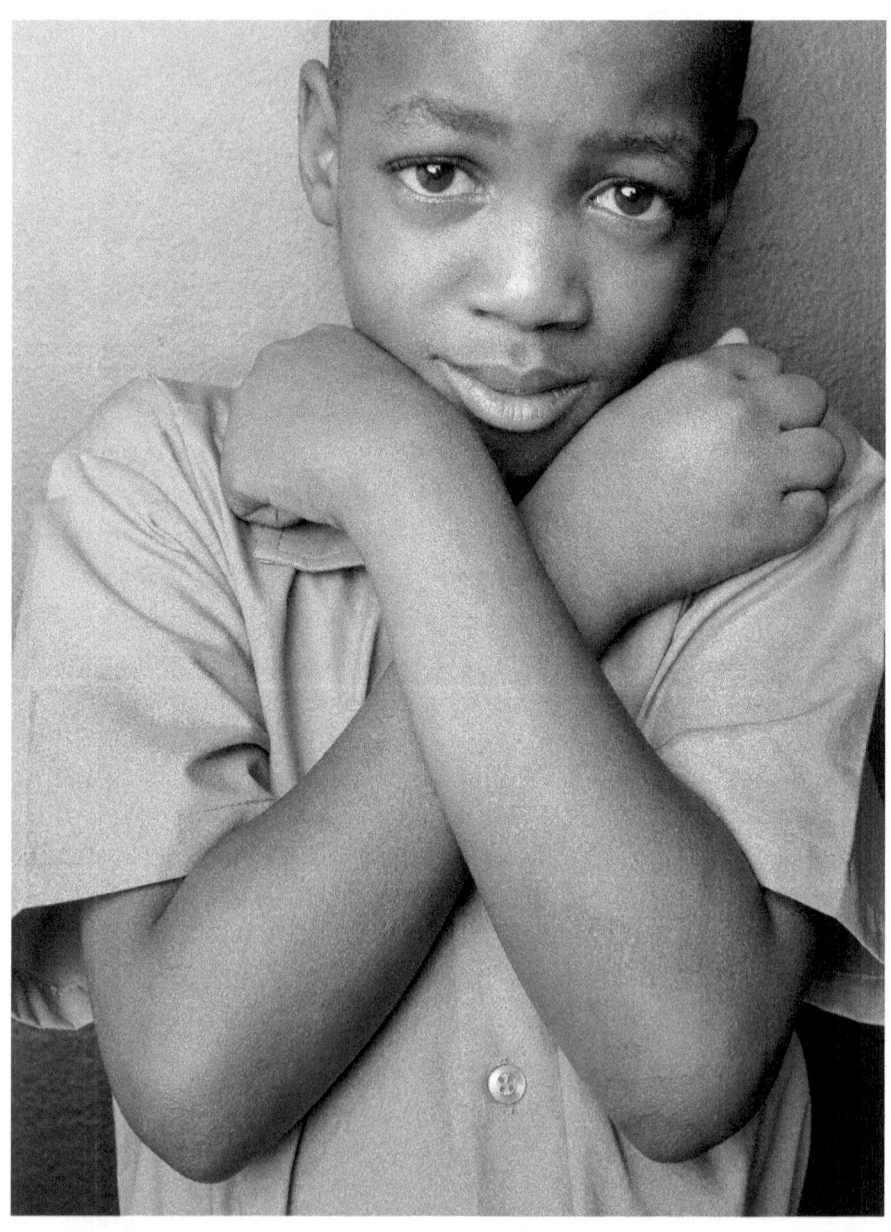

Winning Poems

2nd PRIZE

THE DAY I STOPPED RAISING MY HAND

By Zachary Andrade (15 years old)

I used to raise my hand up high,
like sunlight stretching through the sky.
Eager voice, a burning flame,
unaware of shame or name.

Miss Taylor smiled – "You're bright," she said,
but chose the quiet kid instead.
And when I answered far too fast,
she'd purse her lips and glance right past.

Liam's words were "sharp and deep."
Mine were "loud," or "just a leap."
He was praised, while I got "tone,"
like intellect should stay at home.

At lunch they called my hair a "cloud,"
they laughed at food that smelled too proud.
Jollof rice – a burst of spice –
mocked with grins, not once but twice.

I told Miss T – she brushed it clean,
"They're curious, it's not that mean."
No space to cry, no chance to speak,
my pride grew quieter every week.

Black in White

She read our scores in front of class –
Liam's eighty? "Gold star, brass!"
Mine was ninety-two, no lie –
she blinked, then let the moment die.

I stopped raising my hand that day,
tucked my thoughts and tucked my way.
Buried answers deep inside,
where hurt and doubt and shame reside.

Years passed, I found the words at last –
those "harmless" cuts that shaped my past.
They weren't just jokes, or slips, or stings –
they clipped the roots of growing wings.

But now I write, and now I stand,
this poem raised like that same hand.
For every child who's told to sit –
your voice was born too brightly lit.

Defining Moment: Overt Racism

Overt racism or **explicit racism** is the intentional and/or obvious harmful attitudes or behaviours towards another minority individual or group because of the colour of his/her skin. Overt racist actions are those that are the easiest to see and describe as racism, unlike the more insidious, or covert forms of racism.

- Includes any speech or behaviours that demonstrate a conscious acknowledgement of racist attitudes and beliefs.
- Rooted in white supremacy ideology, which it seeks to reinforce and maintain
- Distinguished by blatant use of negative attitudes, ideas, actions directed at non-white racial groups
- Can be practiced by individuals, groups, institutions, and across societies
- Recently there has been a rise of overtly racist incidents, such as hate crimes corresponding to the election of President Trump.

Source: Fitchburg State University – Amelia V. Gallucci-Cirio Library – Anti-racism Resources

Black in White

Winning Poems

3RD PRIZE

SWEETS TOOK ON A DIFFERENT MEANING
By Jenny Mitchell

When I was a child, everything cost two pee,
coins made out of chocolate melting on my tongue,
stuck out in the playground close to school,
coats thrown on the ground despite December's chill,
ice lollies craved by children soft as jelly babies
cradled on the swings, all-sorts down the slides
until a gang of boys – pale as milky bars –
chant behind the fence the quality of streets
is lost, bounty spoilt by us assortments,
called milk chocolate drops.

Too small to answer back, we're chased beyond
the fence, a marathon that ends too soon
because I am a fun-sized pack, cornered on my own
until I see a busy street, galaxy of shoppers
with eyes wide, gob stoppers in their mouths
to hear me cry for help, breath the final toffee
in a Christmas tin until I try to find escape
fizz bombing in the sweetie shop,
counter weighed with jars of fudge, marshmallows
on the shelves next to sweetened shards.

Black in White

The man who sells it all is a brittle bar that snaps,
face a fist of nuts as he shouts, 'Not another
bloody black jack!' He is like the milky bars,
taller than the tallest shelf, breath the stench
of sour balls, laughter sharp as aniseed
when a belt's undone, waved above my head.
I am walnut whipped, broken
biscuit crumbling home, pear drops
falling hard, sun setting on a fondant
England, pink as a bon-bon.

SECTION 6:
Highly Commended Poems 2025

(in alphabetical order by poem title)

A Colour That Won't Wash Off – Muntaha

Diversity Hire – Yvonne Dang

Dreams Folded Quiet – Janhvi

Echoes In An Empty Playground – Princess Opara

Fragmented Existence – Dr G

How Black – Natasha McDonnell-Tanoh

I Know Who I Am – Paarth Aggarwal

My New Colleague – Bill Lythgoe

Prayer – Tavia Panton

She Carries The Silence Differently – Debbie Miller

Speak When Spoken Word – Jebril Umo

The BAME Game – Farnaz Rais

Tuti – Beda Higgins

What I Carry To Work – Ifeoma Q. Opara

Which Allegiance to Which Cunning
– Shannon Clinton-Copeland

Zero Tolerance – Neelam Sharma

Black in White

CATEGORY: CHILDHOOD

A COLOUR THAT WON'T WASH OFF
By Muntaha *

Have you ever stained something,
And no matter how hard you scrubbed, it just won't leave?

When I was born, my parents held me to the sky.
The sun kissed me, and my skin caught the night.
I scrubbed and scrubbed.
But the colour wouldn't wash off.
I guess blessings don't wash off.

At school, Suzie Williams pen erupted in her bag.
An ugly blotch on her pristine white skirt.
She tossed it in the wash, but the stain persisted.
Loud and proud.

A hush.
A giggle. Sliding between the cloakrooms.
A whisper, nipping my ears.
"Her parents must have dropped her in a vat of ink."
And I began to wonder.
Can blessings be washed off?

I searched far and wide for cures.
Ancient rituals, home remedies, scalding soaps.
Some swore by nature. Others, by bleach.
Nothing worked.
I scrubbed and scrubbed.
But the colour wouldn't wash off.

Highly Commended Poems

Ink seeps.
It does not ask permission. It bleeds into everything you own.
Stains it.
Hair so wild, accent too thick, bangles annoyingly loud.
My laugh took up too much space it seemed.
So, I did the only thing I could do.
If I couldn't wash off the stain.
I'd toss everything it touched.

My coils that reached for the sky I once touched, were flattened.
Silence became my perfume.
No need for gaudy gold. Blasted bangles.
I swallowed my vowels, speaking soft, moving slow.
I was fine to tuck my rhythm away into tighter clothes.
For a while, the whispers stopped. Or maybe I stopped listening.
But then, for just a moment, I turned around.

The same girls that would whisper.
Now golden from bottled sun.
Their hair, a messy crown I once wore. Now beachy waves.
Effortless, chic.
Their wrists clinked and chimed with stacked bangles, sounding like home.
The pieces of me I long discarded, they picked up like treasure.
They looked foreign, but when stood together, I knew they would never feel it.

I stood there. Bare and bleached.
The ink was never the problem.
Only who wore it.
The sun kissed me when I was born.
Forget the ink, I should have worn my skin as the blessing it always was.

* *Pen name*

DIVERSITY HIRE
By Yvonne Dang

CATEGORY: Workplace

I thought that when I grew up, the racism would stop –
still, it persisted (though there was a drop).
What shocked me was it even extended
to work – where I thought such behaviour ended.

I've been lucky early in my career
to not be worried or even fear
that my face or name would hold me back.
Though connections I did lack!

The stereotype of a career in law:
is: 'male, pale and stale' (so, a bit of a bore).
My experience backs that up for sure.
Now this is where things get a bit raw.

I recall mix-ups with a colleague
(also of East Asian descent)
that occurred so much, it caused fatigue
although probably well-meant.

That's usually the excuse, right?
Or do we get an apology for them not being bright?
It's not a matter of intellect though
just a few moments to really get to know

the individuals they see more than those
at home. The lack of effort just shows!
If my surname was "Smith" or "Green"
I'm sure IT would have actually seen

the difference. With two surnames that rhyme with "bang"
they joked: "They must've done
that on purpose!" Those words rang
on my first day like we were recruited for fun.

Or maybe I was just a diversity quota…
But I remained stony faced as if it was poker.
It took too long for me to get my foot in the door
so even if I was just a number, I wasn't going to keep score.

Black in White

> CATEGORY: CHILDHOOD

DREAMS FOLDED QUIET

By Janhvi [Childhood] (15 years old)

I was just a child
who wanted to draw my name in the sky –
in white chalk on a blue board of clouds.
But they handed me grey.
Said, the white would stain.

I was just a child
who folded dreams like paper planes –
hoping they'd reach the sunlit sill.
But the wind was still.
And the air, too thick for wings.

I was just a child
who hummed songs from storybooks read –
in lullaby notes the colours sang.
But the chorus never rang.
They turned down the volume instead.

I was just a child
who carved thrones from mud and thread –
wore crowns of foil with royal flair.
But they wouldn't dare
let my footprints stain their spread.

I was just a child
who knocked at a door with painted glass –
heart in hand, no mask to wear.
But silence filled the air.
And no one told me not all dreams pass.

I knocked like a child, I hoped like a child –
but I left with my name folded quiet and wild.

CATEGORY: CHILDHOOD

ECHOES IN AN EMPTY PLAYGROUND
By Princess Opara (16 years old)

I have walked long shadows,
measured time by the spaces where laughter never reached –
where the games were played but the rules were whispered in code,
spoken in a language only some were taught,
and others, like me, were left to decipher through the ache of exclusion –
a silent cipher, a puzzle of absence in the corners of sunlight.

Why must a child learn to wear invisibility like a second skin,
soft as moth wings but sharp as shattered glass?
To become a ghost among the living – seen only when suspicion falls,
when eyes sharpen like knives, slicing through the air,
tracing every step, every breath, as if my presence was trespassing –
a fault line beneath the polished surface of a schoolyard,
cracked and trembling with unspoken fears.

I was the lone brown boy on the cracked tarmac,
the one never chosen first, nor last with kindness –
always an afterthought, a shadow flickering at the edge of a team
that never wanted me to win.
Is this what freedom looks like?
To stand, uncalled, unclaimed, beneath a sun that lights others but leaves me cold?
Like a wilted leaf, forgotten on the path of a careless footfall.

Highly Commended Poems

Teachers held rulers but not justice –
measuring not my mind but the shade of my skin,
dismissing effort with a flicker of impatience –
demanding silence when my voice rose to explain
that a lesson I learned was not from books, but from scorn.
Their eyes, cold and calculating, carved me smaller,
their words falling like stones, heavy with neglect.

I was punished twice – once by a deed,
once by the colour I carried like a brand burned into my flesh;
my mistakes magnified, their echoes louder
than the whispers excusing the children clad in pale innocence.
Who polices the pain of the unseen?
Who listens when the smallest boy cries out for fairness
and hears instead the chill of indifference,
an empty room echoing with the absence of mercy?

In classrooms devoid of mirrors, I searched for reflection,
only to find heroes with faces as blank as snow –
their stories scripted without me,
as if I belonged only to the margins,
to footnotes of history erased,
to futures prewritten by someone else's hand –
a narrative where my voice was a whisper lost in the roar of the crowd.

I was watched too closely – like a fault waiting to break,
followed through aisles where suspicion marked my every move,
a constant shadow tethered to my heels –
not for what I had done,
but for the skin I could not shed –
a cloak heavier than any winter's night.

Black in White

I learned to speak less freely,
to flatten my accent until it was unrecognizable even to my own tongue,
to fold my culture into pockets too small for its breadth,
to shrink my laughter until it echoed only inside my chest –
a caged bird singing a muted song.

And what of the weight this bore?
The quiet unravelling – the slow corrosion
of a child's belief that they were whole,
that they were worthy beyond the reach of hatred?
Can a young heart survive when each day is a battle –
each smile a fragile shield
against the acid drip of prejudice?

Does a child forget the sting of "You don't belong"?
The laughter that lingers in corridors long after the bell,
the absence of friends invited to celebrations,
the coldness of glances that say: "You are other,"
as if difference is a fault, a fracture in a seamless world?

I ask you – how many children must carry this burden
before the world wakes to the cost of its silence?
How many futures must be trimmed,
how many dreams folded away like forbidden books,
before we decide that this inheritance of pain is ours to end?

And yet –
I hold a fierce hope in the marrow of my bones –
a fire kindled by the faces of children rising now,
speaking in tongues that refuse erasure,
carrying names like flags into the classrooms,
the playgrounds, the spaces that once tried to silence them –
they are not echoes of the past,
but the thunder of change,
a rising tide that will not be contained.

They will not fold themselves away in shadow –
nor will they learn to carry invisibility like a gift –
but will cast off chains forged by ignorance and fear,
dancing beneath skies wide enough to hold every story,
every shade, every voice that has been muted for too long.

I watch them –
brave and unyielding,
their eyes lit with the knowledge that belonging is not a favour,
but a right carved by courage and love.

And to those who cannot know this pain –
who walk untouched by suspicion,
whose lives are never marked by the colour of their skin –

I offer no forgiveness.
Only the fierce truth that their comfort was bought
on the backs of those children who are still learning
how to stand, how to speak, how to be seen.

So listen –
listen to the silence that screams between the lines,
to the footsteps trailing behind,
to the voices rising from forgotten corners.

And then act.
Because the playground is not an empty stage –
It is the world that will inherit us all.

> **CATEGORY: CHILDHOOD**

FRAGMENTED EXISTENCE
*By Dr G ***

Questions repeatedly invaded
about my racialised authenticity.
Judgement against being wholly Black
based primarily on absence of poverty.

Fragments of my existence,
Black but rejected.
Not white, so subjected
to vitriol countering enforced persistence.

Veneer of success in white spaces
Masked searing hurt behind presented faces.
Unrecognised pain for parental gain
whilst observers equated fight with trying to be white.

Questions unasked,
was I healthy within?
Multiple languages without tools to fully decode,
unacknowledged whilst suffering.

Fragments of my existence,
speaking socially within contrasting colours.
Never fluent in affluence or malodorous effluence,
so attacked dually, recurrently.

Veneer of honours in white spaces
whilst losing faces
of self by stealth
for prospects of future wealth.

Dialects spoken simultaneously informs the astute
though decades away, remain persistent.
Seemingly disjointed words completion of authenticity
reflecting fragmented existence.

Pen name

Black in White

CATEGORY: CHILDHOOD

HOW BLACK

By Natasha McDonnell-Tanoh

School was big
Those boys made it small
Nowhere to hide,
Everywhere to hide.

They found me in the corridor, the stairs, the canteen, the walk home
They found me when they weren't even looking
Their words always in whispers,
Quiet and fast

Fat
Your skin is like bird sh*t
Your skin is like cat sh*t
Aren't you a bit big for a starving African?
Fat

Whispers,
Quiet and fast.
To me, loud and ringing
Had I really heard that?
Had the wind delivered the wrong message to the wrong ears?

My sanity in question
One of them emerges in the corridor alone
I am alone.
A deep laugh rises from his stomach spilling out of his mouth, bouncing off the walls

Highly Commended Poems

Black fatty
Wait, are you even Black?
How are you Black?
How Black are you?

He's stepping forward
I step back
My head hung
He holds my dignity in his palm

I am 11 years old
I am curved
My posture slowly becoming the letter C
Forming a protective cave for my heart

In that moment I wish my skin to become the shade of the deep evening
My heart to pump black blood
My tears to be black ink
So black inside and out that this question never again finds me
This self-rejection is an injection of guilt

Roots sprout from my toes and burrow through the concrete ground
Through the soil
To the very centre of the earth
Rooted

HOW Black are you?
He squeezes my dignity in his white hand
His gummy smile expanding as I stay rooted to the spot

Black in White

Rooted and curved
Ashamed and strong
Leaves sprout from my skin
Roots continue to grow from my toes

His head thrown back spilling more laughter
He leaves
With my dignity in his pocket
His words left behind as disregarded rubbish
Laughter still bouncing off the walls

How Black am I?
Guilt gained weight
Shame tightens its grip
I raise my head and go to class

Some-time later I am at the park
Spending time in the grass
More leaves have sprouted from me
Tasting the sun
My skin bark-like
I welcome this transformation
What is more belonging than a tree?

The boys show up
Barking laughter

Fat n*gga
Fat n*gga
Fat n*gga

They chant like werewolves howling at the full moon
Am I the full moon?
Their laughter like lashes
This time they do not whisper
They roar loudly without the restriction of the school walls

*Fat n*gga*
*Fat n*gga*
*Fat n*gga*

I can't control my water
Rivers cascade from my eyes
Some of my leaves become limp
Some carried away by the wind

At least I know that today
I am Black enough to be considered a n*gga

> CATEGORY: Workplace

I KNOW WHO I AM

By Paarth Aggarwal (16 years old)

They called me names I didn't know,
Then laughed when I looked down –
Like being different was a joke
In this pale-painted town.

They said my skin was "too much sun,"
My lips, my nose, my hair –
Like beauty came in only shapes
That I would never wear.

They told me, "Speak like you belong,"
But I was always me –
My voice holds oceans, roots, and storms
That won't bow to a sea.

They said, "You're not like all the rest,"
As if that was a prize.
But I could see the lie they held
Still dancing in their eyes.

At first, I tried to scrub it off -
My name, my voice, my shade.
Until I saw the magic in
The things they tried to fade.

Highly Commended Poems

I come from warriors, song and stone,
From poets, drums, and flame.
And I will not make myself small
To fit inside their frame.

So let them whisper, point, or scoff –
I've heard it all before.
But every time they shut a gate,
I build a brighter door.

I know the power in my walk,
The fire in my skin.
And no one gets to dim the light
I carry deep within.

CATEGORY: Workplace

MY NEW COLLEAGUE

By Bill Lythgoe

A big, proud Black man,
a refugee whose name is Luba.
I've seen him around
but don't know his story.

When I ask where he's from
he stares at me
and lets me see
he's been asked this too many times before:

Congo Zaire, if you know where that is.

Course I know where it is.
it's where Muhammed Ali
fought George Foreman.

His eyes light up:
Ah – I remember that.
I was only a little boy.

I knew there was something
important going on
but I didn't know what it was.

He smiles and shouts:
Ali   Boma ye!

Ali   Boma ye!
My new friend.

Highly Commended Poems

CATEGORY: Workplace

PRAYER

By Tavia Panton

To no supreme god
Do I address my elegy
This is for you in the crowd
Whether you are already Black and proud
Or on your journey of self-discovery
This prayer is our recovery
From oppressive, draining explanations
To save ourselves, say no, damn expectations
Time is a colonial construct
So is race, so is hard work, instruct
Schools of child labour
Attracting philanthropic white saviours to create
Apprenticeship, indentureship
Chained in the belly of the ship
To the plantation
This is my proclamation
To dismantle enduring mental bonds
From Liverpool across the Atlantic pond

Heritage refers to the things we value from our past
And the harder lessons whose impressions last
I pray that we remember the burdens and the peaks
Evolve mistakes into lessons and share our blessings
After the deep damage of Europe's fingers in Africa is repaired
After the known truth is unequivocally declared
I ask for peace, a conscious satisfaction
In spaces where stress could be our only reaction
And I pray that we all act accordingly

Black in White

Following just minds supportively
Don't just smile with the placid folk
Anti-racism, decolonisation, our lives are not a joke
Welcome those in who've previously been pushed out
Avoid corporate language so our intentions don't fall to doubt
Show everyone there's care, respect humanity right
Treat me like I'm precious but save room for my dynamite
Slavery Remembrance Day is how
We recognise the captivity we have overthrown
It helps us understand how we live now
And where we could end up when we're grown

Highly Commended Poems

CATEGORY: Workplace

SHE CARRIES THE SILENCE DIFFERENTLY
By Debbie Miller

They praised her diction
called it "articulate,"
as if her tongue
had borrowed excellence
from elsewhere.
She moved through glass corridors
like wind in a closed room
present, but never
quite seen the way
she saw herself reflected.
Her name
shortened without consent
rested on their lips
like an inconvenience.
They didn't ask.
They just rebranded.
Ideas once hers
blossomed in other mouths,
tended by hands
that never knew the root.
Laughter at the edge of meetings
carried undertones she heard
but wasn't meant to.
A dialect of dismissal

spoken in nods and narrowed eyes.
Still, she stayed
not out of comfort,
but courage.
She was not there to belong.
She was there to outlast
the forgetting.

Highly Commended Poems

> **CATEGORY: CHILDHOOD**

SPEAK WHEN SPOKEN WORD

By Jebril Umo (17 years old)

I. Classroom Echoes
They said I was quiet.
Not shy but silent in a way that unsettled them.
As if my tongue was a grenade pin, they couldn't see,
worried what'd happen if I finally *spoke freely*.
So they gave me words. Simple ones.
Nice. Loud. Disruptive.
None that fit, but all that stuck.
And I learned early: Labels don't need glue when sewn into your skin.

II. Accent Wars
"Can you not speak properly?"
Translation: Can you not bury your roots when I look at you?
As if I can't say "mandem" and still master metaphors.
Like rhythm and grammar can't dance in the same breath.
They don't hear the poetry in how I switch tongue like gears.
Like *bruv* and *therefore* ain't cousins.

III. Gifted
They asked what I wanted to be.
I said: *A writer.*
They paused.
Not hostile, just… surprised.
Like ambition was a language they never expected me to speak.
I saw it. In their eyes.
The quiet way they rewrote me: not future novelist, but "rapper."
Not thinker, but "creative."
As if brilliance only belongs when it rhymes.

IV. Response
So, I write now.
Not to prove but to plant.
Each line a seed that splits concrete.
Each poem a classroom they can't control.
I write so the next Black boy won't have to shrink just to survive the curriculum.

Highly Commended Poems

CATEGORY: Workplace

THE BAME GAME
By Farnaz Rais

Let's play a game
You know, THE game
The one where we smile politely when they misspell your name
The name that's written in your email
The name that they continue to mispronounce
Even after you've explained.

Let's play a game
The one where we sigh when we're asked where we're from, where we're really from
When they've already placed us in the 'United Republic of BAME'
That wild place where all the Black and brown folk aren't tame
The lands where savages eat with their hands
Where we waited 'til our white saviours came.

Let's play a game
The one where we grit our teeth when they say we are all the same
That there's no difference between our kings and our queens and our food and our art and music and our languages and our…
Pain
And what unites us is they stole from our lands and our people
And now it's ignorance that they claim.

Let's play a game
The one where we call out micro as macroaggressions
Where we speak on the truth, the trauma, the blame
Where this angry brown woman embraces the slur
And reclaims the power from ashes and flames
And stands tall without fear or shame.

CATEGORY: CHILDHOOD

TUTI

By Beda Higgins

I don't like crowds
Lots of people make me nervous, so fate
pops me in London, lonely and afraid
staring at high-rise flats instead of mountains.

I like the outdoors and wild spaces.
Boxed-in behind slit-eyed windows
grimy with the daily grind of living, there is
a momentous effort to get out of bed.

At the refugee centre, they give me a map
and point to a patch of green. I find it and
follow a path to sit under a park tree.
Daily, strangers nod as if I do exist.

Branches point to the same sky as when
I was seven and climbed the highest.
The lake ripples and rocks me gently
cradling the hours.

Every day, I choose a stone,
rub it clean, and launch it far as I can
skimming across the water.
It skips oceans, and for a moment

      I am home.

Highly Commended Poems

CATEGORY: Workplace

WHAT I CARRY TO WORK

By Ifeoma Q. Opara (17 years old)

I carry more than a bag into work each morning.
I carry code-switches folded like handkerchiefs in my chest pocket –
my voice recalibrated to sound less... threatening,
my curls tamed, my earrings small, my dialect ironed crisp
like the shirt I chose not for style but for survival.

I sip tea in the break room, nod at the jokes –
laugh just enough to be polite, not too much to stand out.
And when I offer a thought in a meeting, it floats –
ignored – until a white voice wraps it in clarity
and suddenly, it's "brilliant."

They don't hear me. Not really.
Am I invisible? Or just inconvenient?

They say, "You're so articulate!"
As though my grammar is a costume I borrowed.
As though fluency in my own tongue surprises them
like a trick dog dancing on cue.
They ask, "Where are you really from?"
And I want to scream – Right here! Right here!
But I've learned that answering feels like confessing.

I have watched my ideas dismissed,
only to bloom in another's mouth.
My labour praised – on someone else's lapel.

Black in White

How many times have I been passed over
for promotions without reason,
for roles with no explanation,
for praise I earned but never held?
How many times have I seen men, lesser than me in merit,
Rise – while I remain their shadow?

Why am I always the "diversity" on the panel,
the one to lead Black History Month – unpaid,
unrecognised, overburdened by inclusion that excludes?

They parade me in photos – our workplace "looks" diverse –
but ask me behind closed doors to quiet down.
To "not take it personally."
To smile more.
To stop seeing race in everything.

But race sees me before I step into the building.
It follows me into performance reviews
where my "tone" is noted,
where my "confidence" is "too much,"
where my "ambition" is "concerning."

I am watched when I walk in.
And watched when I walk out.
My mistakes amplified.
My success treated like an exception.

I hear them whisper.
That I got this job for ticking boxes.
That I don't deserve to be here.
That I should be grateful.

Well, let me be clear.
I did not crawl through doors just to be
held at the threshold.

I am more than a badge in your HR report.
I am brilliance buried beneath your ignorance.
I am resilience shaped into elegance.

Still –
I am tired.
Of smiling through offence.
Of whispering truth into rooms that echo with silence.
Of explaining why your microaggressions feel like stings
because they are stings – repetitive, quiet, and designed to bleed without
bruises.

Do you think we don't notice?
The lunches we're not invited to?
The inside jokes we don't get?
The meetings held after hours,
the golf course deals we were never meant to hear about?

Do you think we don't see it?
That when we enter, you exit warmth?

I want rest.
But not the kind that forgets.
The kind that builds.

I want space.
Not offered – but earned.
Without compromise.

Black in White

I want my daughters to work
without wondering if their name
on a CV is a liability.

I want my son to wear his voice
without it being seen as a threat.

I want equity – not decoration.

I have carried this silence for decades.
Worn this double consciousness like a second uniform.
But not anymore.

Because I was not made for erasure.
And I was not born to prove my place.

Highly Commended Poems

CATEGORY: CHILDHOOD

WHICH ALLEGIANCE TO WHICH CUNNING

By *Shannon Clinton-Copeland*

After *'Black Allegiance to the Cunning'* by Lynette Yiadom-Boakye, oil on linen, 2018

Floor cold as late October,
waxed like a body shining, like a
pageant girl. Kitchen floor as chessboard.
Kitchen floor as capital. This is the ideal
kitchen floor for raising yourself from
the trap of your class, the trap
of your colour, just remember – every trap
asks something. Begs a limb. You may
slip into the forest child and live if
you leave a paw to convince
the hunter you are lying somewhere, dying somewhere
in the brush. Play the game

                         of the floor. There are no
mixed terms for this. Lines clear cut
as diamonds into diamonds. Be
careful.

These are all points on which
you can cut yourself escaping from
the traps of your birth. This floor asks you
for a binary allegiance like the chessboard does – tap your clock,
the time has been running while you
have been panting your hours
tearing your foot from the claw,

Black in White

    this is
          necessary work,
the floor is polished to such a sparkle
it will reflect division into your dreams and
you will never
think in sepia tones again.
Be quick, but not too quick,
decide what is
              worth losing,
what piece will you give, what
     line will you cross,
what line will cross you out,
what chair leg will bear down
on you, is the proof
                worth the pudding is the
pelt worth dying for decide
    the size of your morals
    the width of your conscience
    the makeup of your cunning
    the trap

is asking and when has it ever taken no for an answer,
    what can you let go of, what
    limb of history are you willing to sever which
    children for a drum which
    child for the dinner which
    king for the digestif which
    crop for one more winter which
    mother for a scapegoat
    which island to the
    hungry maw
            where
            does your allegiance lie
            is it truthful

is it with bedfellows who
                would skin you in your sleep
                just for some occupation

will you give the fields, the mazes, the cairns
the breadfruit, the ackee, the patois half-learned you

are bleeding out
something has to go
which language
which accent
be smart   about it
be cunning   the floor
is grinning for a spill   the earth
is turning your dead over what

   is the worth of your coat   the worth
of your prized colour

                what

                        can you give to us

                what

    can we add
to the cabinet of treasures today

ZERO TOLERANCE

By Neelam Sharma

CATEGORY: Workplace

'We are proudly diverse,'
declares the trust pillar,
'empathy and compassion,'
for our patients and staff
to treat everyone fairly so we feel
'valued and appreciated'
with opportunities for all.
And when a patient throws a racist slur
and colleagues trip over racial stereotypes,
there are systems in place:
zero tolerance for abuse,
a Freedom to Speak up Guardian.
So, I do. When a senior staff member
describes the EDL as a cultural nationalist group
with football allegiances,
to an almost entirely global majority staff group,
astounded by his comfort to do so
and not called out by the white lead,
I complain about his comment
ill-judged and unhelpful at best,
or a paid-up member of the terrorist group?
And the director listens, understands,
quotes the chief nursing officer:
'There is no place for racism in the NHS…'
He speaks to the man's manager and HR,
asks what outcome I would like,
unconscious bias training might be a start.
You see we empower people to complain.

But then I'm asked if I'd like a meeting
with this man to explain what my
problem is with his definition.
Why people of colour do not feel safe
when the EDL march on their road
projecting hate with shouts and rocks,
attacking hotels with asylum seekers
peeking through net curtains and smashed
windows. Why they feel uncomfortable
travelling through an area where chairs
are hurled, petrol bombs set off,
to get to work in a hospital. Because
of course it is my responsibility
to make him understand
the problem with his remark.
Would that be me meeting with two white men
to explain my problem with his description,
which he'll say was taken from a credible source,
where he tells me I didn't understand his meaning
his intention to reassure,
his definition of why the EDL are not
a far-right Islamophobic terrorist group.
That I'm overreacting –
I decline.
We are proudly diverse…

Defining Moment: Racism

Racism is discrimination, prejudice or malicious acts towards individuals or communities because of skin colour, ethnicity, nationality, language, customs or practices and place of birth.

Source: University of York – Glossary of EDI Terminology – Race and ethnicity

SECTION 7:

About The Transforming Words Foundation

Black in White

No matter what people tell you, words and ideas can change the world.

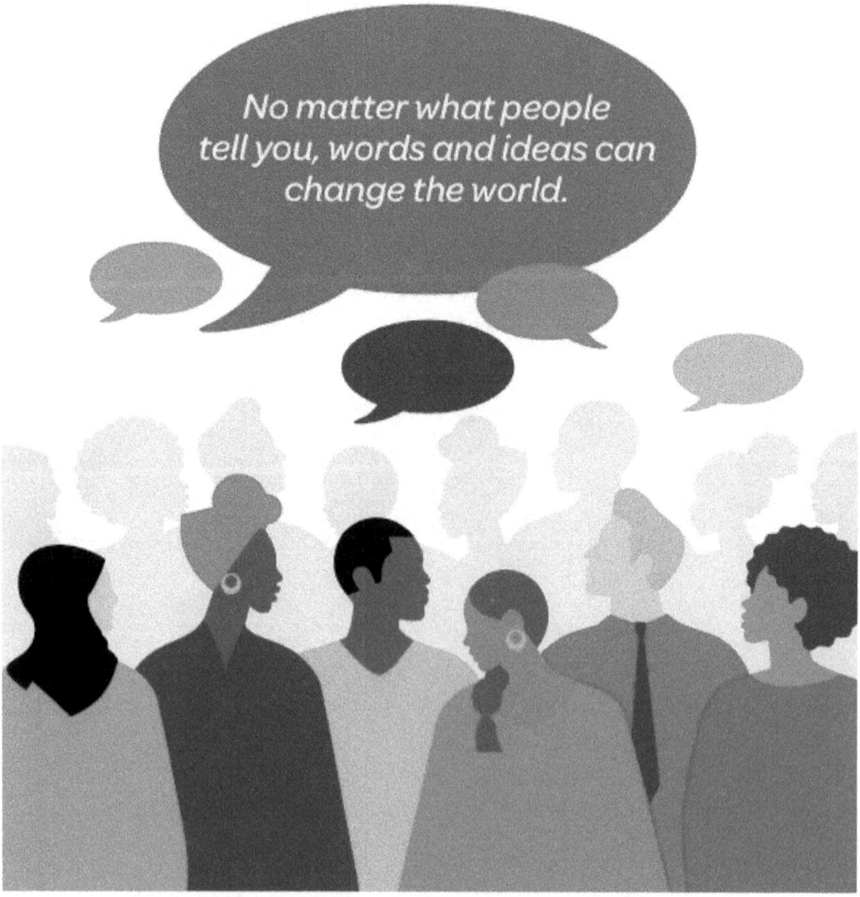

Registered Charity Number: 1213798

About TTWF

Know Us

The Transforming Words Foundation (TTWF) is a charity (Registered Charity Number: 1213798) that has evolved from the social enterprise Black in White, which was founded in 2020 by poet and DEI expert Charlotte Shyllon. Over the last five years, the team has successfully run annual poetry competitions, which attract a wide demographic of people of all ages and backgrounds who resonate with the ability to express their experiences through poetry.

Containing poems by Charlotte and the winning and highly commended poetry competition entrants, five poetry collections have been published to date. These delve into the profound impacts of prejudice, racism, and unconscious bias experiences, which affect people of all ages, in the workplace and in childhood. Through creative expression, we aim to empower individuals, build resilience, break barriers, foster understanding and contribute to positive social change.

Building on this foundation, TTWF carries forward the vision of *sharing stories and shaping societies.* Our mission is to amplify the voices of those who have been marginalised, providing the tools and platforms to express their experiences through creative writing, visual interpretation and spoken word. We believe in the power of words as catalysts for change and healing and we are committed to fostering a world where every voice is heard, understood and valued.

Our Board of Trustees comprises four experienced individuals, Keith Aki-Sawyerr, Annette Fisher, Dean McCarthy and Tanya von Ahlefeldt. Our committed Executive Leaders are Chief Executive Officer Charlotte Shyllon, and Chief Operating Officer Jacqueline Muili. The TTWF team also has several amazing volunteers who play a key role in helping to plan and implement our activities and initiatives. They are David, Debbie, Georgia, Hanna, Lucy, Marcia, Marvelle and Sarah.

Understand Us

Our mission

To create safe spaces where creativity serves as a powerful tool for healing, resilience, and social change. We empower individuals to confront and express experiences with racism, prejudice and personal challenges by using written, spoken and visual communication. We illuminate the impact of racism, celebrate all forms of diversity, and inspire the transformation of minds, hearts and lives.

Our vision

A world where every voice is heard, understood, and valued through the transformative power of words. We envision a future where creative expression is accessible to all, bridging divides, promoting healing and fostering a global culture of empathy and inclusion.

Our core values

Inclusivity, Empowerment, Social Justice, Resilience.

Our strategic priorities

- ❖ We dream of widening the circle, in rooms and online, where stories can be shared. Workshops, outreach, and schools will open new doors for expression.
- ❖ We want our work to matter deeply. By listening closely and learning carefully, we'll shape programmes that truly touch lives.
- ❖ To keep the flame burning, we'll nurture many streams of support. Donors, grants and new ideas will carry our mission into the future.
- ❖ We'll let the world know that creativity heals and empowers. Through voices raised, partnerships formed and messages shared, our story will travel far.

Support Us

This is a pivotal moment for us. By supporting TTWF, you are investing in a future where voices that have been silenced find the strength to speak, heal and inspire others. Join us in creating spaces where words become a tool for empowerment, and every story shared lights the way to a more just and compassionate world.

Donate

We need funds to be able to undertake the various activities we have outlined in our strategic plan. If you would like to make a regular or one-time donation to support our work, please use one of the options below:

- **Website:** long onto our website, www.ttwf.org.uk, and click the red 'Donate' button
- **Easyfundraising**: log onto www.easyfundraising.org.uk and search for The Transforming Words Foundation

Volunteer

We are looking for people who share our vision to join our team. To become a volunteer, send your CV to info@ttwf.org.uk.

Black in White

The Transforming Word Foundation's Chairman Keith Aki-Sawyerr was inspired to write a limerick about our four Trustees; they are: Keith (a civil engineer turned entrepreneur), Dean (a family law solicitor), Tanya (a strategic communications specialist) and Annette (an award-winning architect). Enjoy!

The Transforming Words Foundation's the name,
Awareness and resilience - the aim.
We foster great change,
With impact wide-range,
No community we touch stays the same

Trustees of the Foundation are four,
They bring talent and insight galore:
There's Keith with bold schemes,
Dean's justice redeems,
While Tanya and Annette explore!

The Foundation has a plan,
To uplift so others may learn.
Sharing stories around,
Shaping societies un-browned,
To inspire a bold resilient clan.

© Keith Aki-Sawyerr, 2025

Contact Us

E: info@ttwf.org.uk

W: www.ttwf.org.uk

Facebook: The Transforming Words Foundation

Instagram: @transformingwordsfoundation

LinkedIn:

www.linkedin.com/company/the-transforming-words-foundation/

"Sharing Stories, Shaping Societies"